SOCIETY
AT THE
CROSSROADS

Nelson N.K.

SOCIETY
AT THE
CROSSROADS

Nelson N.K.

DORRANCE PUBLISHING CO
EST. 1920
PITTSBURGH, PENNSYLVANIA 15238

Dorrance Publishing Co
585 Alpha Drive
Pittsburgh, PA 15238
Visit our website at www.dorrancebookstore.com

ISBN: 978-1-6461-0175-7
eISBN: 978-1-6461-0533-5

This might not seem like your ordinary note-book, but it is all there is to say. Therefore, take a deep breath and read…then think about it… then read again…. for your understanding is all there is…

I thank you all for taking your busy time to listen for its always important to be informed.

INTRODUCTION

The presidential tenure is almost over. As the country is busy preparing for the next election, many questions still linger in many people's minds as to what happened during the previous election. There are more questions than answers provided to the society today explaining as to what might have led to the historic outcome of the previous election in 2016. Many in the society from near and far are confused, not knowing what to do or expect next.

What many need to understand is that the constitution of this great country sets basic guidelines as to who qualifies to be the president of the United States of America. The constitution never said that anyone can only be the president of this country based on the approval of a specific individual or based on approval of a group of individuals, neither does the constitution of this country say that to be the president of this country will require Congressional, senatorial, or even the judicial approval. All the constitution says is that if you can meet the set up criteria required to run for the president of this country, then you can be elected by the public of this country and be the ultimate leader of this society: the President of the United States of America.

Therefore many are all wondering, where is the feud between the society leaders coming from? Don't you know that you may all be fighting with anger and therefore might end up fighting with your own self unknowingly!

It is the entire society that matters the most and not a specific individual within the society and that is what all leaders of this great country and the world at large need to understand and contemplate first.

To many in the United States of America political circle, what happened in 2016 may just be another day occurrence. A new leader comes in and everyone starts adjusting to the new leadership as usual. But to the poor, and especially those who depend on the United States of America for guidance, the outcome of that election was a very big deal, a deal so big that could not be ignored at all cost and that was why many from all walks of life. Rich and poor took to the streets demanding reasonable explanation as to what had just happened. Why the unexpected outcome? What is going on? That is why the country chose a special counsel to investigate to find the truth in the bid to satisfy the public's demands.

Today as we speak, the investigation is over but provided hardly any feasible answer to the public as to what may have happened during that election year leaving many bewildered, many wondering as to why they had to wait eagerly for so long only to be told that nothing out of the ordinary happened, leaving many to believe that the investigation was just another government conspiracy to hide the truth from the public. For this reason, I chose to take this valuable moment to substantiate the facts from fiction and the truth from heresy as to what exactly happened and also why.

UNITED STATES OF AMERICA SOCIETY

The society in the United States of America is very unique in the sense that it comprises of three distinct groups or categories of individuals, other than visitors and illegal immigrants. First are the individuals within the society who are born on the United States of America's soil such that this country is their only and only home come rain or sunshine. Second are the individuals who have gained citizenship through immigration and now call this country their only home. Thirdly are many others with residency and dual citizenship such that this country is their home but they still have another home somewhere else. They who haven't made up their mind yet as to which will be their better home. Many in transition of becoming full blown citizens of the United States of America but just taking their sweet time and not in any rush. That is why this country is said to be the country of immigrants.

During the early ages of the development of the society of this country, there came the need for the society to have one law of the land. The constitution that unites all under one roof so that all living in this country can operate under the guidance of one order. This was necessary because, as Grandma said, a society can only operate in peace while under one law and hence one order. For whenever the second or third order steps in, confrontation and "war" is bound to follow because of the confusion that emerges. A society under one rule, one law, and one leadership is always unconfused and hence works in perfect unison effortlessly.

The constitution of this country was designed and meant to offer a flamework, a skeleton, or basic guideline through which all other laws of the land should follow or attach to. All other laws have to lime or be in agreement with the constitutional order. Therefore, the constitution left many gray areas upon which the lawmakers of the land can fill in with many other laws based on the changing society of this nation. Thereby giving the lawmakers enough room to operate in while dealing with the society that was already foreseen to change as time went by.

In this society, per the constitution of the land, the president of the United States of America can only come from the first group, the citizens by birth and not by naturalization. While congress, senate, and even the judicial leaders can be from either group. Also, per the constitution of the land, the president elect can only serve the public for a maximum of two terms.

But why was the constitution written that way, such that the president of the USA can only be someone born in the USA and can only serve for two terms?

It's because the forefathers who labored to concoct this country's constitution could very much predict the possibility of someone very rich and powerful emerging some time later on in time and corrupt the society by using power and money, resulting in anguish, agony, and suffering of many. This was especially so because the country was formulated by societies that migrated from different parts of the planet and hence had varying ideas, beliefs, and values which could very much interfere with the normal working of the new society. Therefore, in order to protect the lives as well as livelihood of those who were to be born in United States of America, the top-most leader had to be from among them, had to be born from United States of America and not a newcomer.

The same forefathers could also see the benefit to the overall society, and especially while the society was in the young stages of development, of recognizing and encompassing other leaders from the incoming societies migrating from all over the world and that is why congress, senate, and the judicial system were left open for any leader to fill in no matter where they originated from, as long as they were elected by the public as dictated by the constitution of the United States of America.

More so it was and still is only the presidential position that the leader can only be in office for a maximum of two terms, thereby allowing other leaders from regions across the planet where leaders stay in office longer to still continue to do so while serving the public of their newly-found home, the United States of America, as long as their constituents elects them back to office each time after four-year term, or as mandated by the constitution of this country.

The main reason as to why the president of the United States of America is supposed to be a citizen of this country by birth is because of the universal saying in all societies that says: EAST OR WEST, HOME IS THE BEST. Home is NOT Just home. Home is the society that someone grows up in since one was born, the society one grows up at since a little child, the society that instills values, morals, ideas, believes, and old-time memories in someone's life since childhood. Hence facilitating someone in developing innate love to that society they live in and therefore always ready to die for their society as well as their country.

To an outsider, someone else's home may be irrelevant, useless, outdated, backward, crazy, undeveloped, or anything else one might want to call it. But to those belonging to that society, that is their only paradise, the only place that provides hope they need and hence cherished by all who live there and many others with close association to that home.

The presidency of the United States of America is not just a title, rather the dedication to serve the people of United States of America and to sustain and promote all of their endeavors. It is the duty and the mission at hand that goes with that title of the president that bears more importance than the individual in question, for an individual can never be of more importance than the whole. However, the quality of the individuals comprising the whole always determine the overall society's performance as the whole is just a combination of many individuals within. That is why better education to all within the society is always emphasized for an educated mind stands a better chance of making great judgments for the society's survival.

As the constitution of this country dictates, the president of United States of America is required to serve the public with undivided attention. For the ultimate leader to accomplish this mandate, the leader must be a citizen of the United States of America by birth. Which means, since east or west home is the best, if the president is a citizen of United States of America by birth, the president's only home will be United States of America and if and only if the president absolutely has no other home, the president should be able to serve the people of United States of America with full attention, undeterred by enemies and with all the might and power handed over to the ultimate leader by the people through fair and free elections per the constitution of this country. The president elect should have no shortage of supply for the better of the country and the society at large.

However, if the president of United States of America is someone else born from another country now a citizen of the United States of America by naturalization, the president will always remember the old home no matter what and hence will not be able to serve the people of United States of America with undivided attention as mandated to do by the constitution of this country.

Nevertheless, the constitution of this country does not prevent someone born in the United States of America who decided to move to another society and gained dual citizenship from running for the president of this country as long as the individual have been a resident of the United States of America for fourteen years prior to the election. However, such an individual stands very little chance of convincing the public as to which home is the best to serve and therefore easily loses the public's trust early during the campaign. The candidate will be incapable of explaining to the public how the leader would be serving the public of United States of America with undivided attention if ever get elected while the candidate already has two masters to serve, two homes. No wonder no candidate holding dual citizenship has ever been elected as the president of this country.

The potential candidate for the president of the United States of America has to be living within the society for the past fourteen years so as to allow the individual in question to fully understand the society the leader is to lead if elected. Grandma said that it is always necessary to be knocking on the door before entering. This means, in this situation, that you as a candidate is supposed to fully understand the society in and out and hence be knowledgeable about the problems the society is facing as well as acquire enough knowledge regarding how the society you live in works before you can even try to consider leading the same society. It takes time to understand societal issues and concerns as they are always complicated and varying. Therefore the forefathers figured out that fourteen years of continuous residency within the society is adequate time for someone to fully understand the society one lives in, establish good working relationship with many in that society, and innately develop unconditional love and trust with the society which would allow the potential candidate to be capable of leading that society successfully and with ease.

It is never the individual that maters the most, rather the whole and the whole is the entire society. Hence any potential candidate for the presidency of the United States of America needs to first develop adequate knowledge, passion, and wisdom relating to the society. Rather than jumping into a fast-moving boat on a busy day, the constitution of this country mandates for any presidential candidate to first test the waters before boarding the ship for the sake of all the passengers on board. That is why all the candidates are required to be part of the society for the past fourteen years prior to the presidential elections.

Per the constitution of the United States of America, the president is supposed to serve in office for only two terms so as to prevent the possibility of a few powerful and rich leaders from controlling the vast majority in the society. Many poor people require guidance and hardly know where and when to turn from right to left and hence can easily be out-manipulated by someone with enough resources, knowledge, and power for undetermined period of time, which might lead to unnecessary anguish to many in the society.

More so, by switching the top leadership you bring in new ideas, new ways of getting things done, new blood, and hence new aid to the society in exploiting all of its human resource potential in order to maximize productivity and therefore propel the country forward at a faster pace for an easier and better tomorrow. That was and still is the basis of democracy: to share power in an organized manner by having the public freely and fairly elect their preferred leaders of their society.

Each leader is required by the constitution of this country to give up that top position, no matter how prestigious it might be, to the next leader after a specific period of time and the incoming leader has to be allowed in by the public through fair and free elections. That is why in a democratic government the leader is required to explain to the public how their burning issue will be better solved if the leader is elected during the campaign trail. Also, per the constitution of United States of America, the outgoing leader is prohibited from going back to office for the rest of their lifetime to allow many other leaders born in this country to enjoy the same opportunity.

The United States of America however is beyond the boundaries that mark the territorial USA. It is combination of the society that lives within the boundaries of United States of America's territory and the vast societies affiliated directly or indirectly to this great country. Very many societies from near and far cherish the United States of America's way of life as well as leadership. As the number one leader in civilized societies, United States of America stands at a unique position unparalleled to any other nation on the face of this planet as an epicenter, a modal for many other countries and societies rich or poor, developed or developing, to follow in their bid to better their tomorrow.

Therefore, when something out of ordinary happens within the boundaries of United States of America, many poor people from near and far are bothered and hence deserve a reasonable explanation from parties involved. This is because the concerns from the society living within this country as well as similar concerns emanating from other societies living outside the boundaries of this country, but have direct relations with the United States of America, are of equal relevance and therefore requires to be addressed with equal urge and integrity for a peaceful and prosperous future for all.

For anyone to claim that what happened in 2016 was just normal or for anyone to ignore the fact that something out of ordinary happened on that day, is just refusing to accept the reality and therefore refusing to learn and grow for a better tomorrow. By ignoring and refusing to accept reality, you end up living in perpetual darkness and might end up inviting history to repeat itself the very next day. It's always important to learn from our mistakes of yesterday for history is said to be the best teacher. However, the only way we can learn from the mistakes we made in the past is by first finding out what happened yesterday so that we all can have a starting point, a lesson to start our school today for a better tomorrow.

The fact is, since when did someone or anyone who is loathed by his own family and hated by his neighbors to their last breath ever became the chosen leader of the clan? May be that might have happened in the past such that what happened in 2016 was just a repetition of history. However one thing is for sure, things like that don't happen just by chance. It is not an everyday occurrence and definitely it is an indication that something was not right or still isn't because for such unusual outcomes to be realized in this society at that specific time, something must have been cooking and the smell was not that pleasant.

What was surprising about the 2016 campaign was that President Donald Trump could even go after the proverbial, the untouchables, "women" sitting in very high ranks in the society as well as high ranking leaders of the entire society, not to mention just about anyone else from all walks of life who attempted to challenge candidate Donald Trump. Even former leaders were all Trump's best enemies in the political arena, whether Democrats or Republicans, and no news reporters were reporting real stuff, only fake made up stories according to candidate Donald Trump. While other previous presidential front runners during the campaign period usually go for advice from their predecessors, Donald Trump was going against former presidents like no one's business and was not even worried about going after highly-respected, retired military icons the society had at that time. This has never happened before in the history of this country and was all news to many in the nation as well as to many throughout global civilized societies.

And of course, as you all can remember, during the entire campaign trail, Donald Trump was never ahead in the polls predicting who stands the best chance to be elected as the next president of the United States of America. Not to mention that Donald Trump actually lost on ALL of the presidential debates against the only opponent remaining on the field, Hilary Clinton. To many in society at large, the entire campaign was like the greatest and most hilarious joke ever. Even to have Donald Trump running for the president of United States of America did not sit too well in the minds of many in the society as well as their well-wishers and friends worldwide. It was like an entertainment for everyone to watch and talk about. Nevertheless, amidst all the talks and laughter, Donald Trump unprecedently ended up winning the election leaving many in dismay.

Therefore, for Donald Trump to end up winning the election and becoming the next president in 2016, something was definitely going on. There had to be another reason to support the outcome, a hidden message important for the society to first understand. Something was not right. It just doesn't happen that way on a normal day in the normal workings of the society. There was something that society needed to address first and fast.

It was not surprising that when Donald Trump was elected as the president of the United States of America, All the president said was that it could have been Russia, China, or anyone else. The president elect was just saying that it could have been Moses or it could have been Joshua or any other massager that got Donald Trump into power because even for the newly elected president, that was a very difficult shot to make and a very, very long way home. The president could very much tell that there must have been a helping hand. It turned out that Donald Trump was on the right as far as Heaven was concerned based on the constitution of this country while Donald Trump's opponent Hilary Clinton was not.

The outcome of this election was overwhelmingly contrary to what many in this country as well as other societies everywhere throughout the planet expected and that is why under the pressure of the people's quest to find out what happened. The unstoppable public outcry from so many poor souls wondering about what may lay ahead that the government assigned a team of experts to unearth all the secretes underlying the extraordinarily unanticipated outcome of the election. An outcome which, to the vast majority and especially many poor souls living elsewhere in the planet, was one hundred percent in conflict to their expectations and beliefs, especially considering when and in which country it happened. For sure, this was their worst nightmare and many can't even believe what happened that day up to this day.

The special council was unanimously approved by the lawmakers to investigate the issue and to thoroughly investigate what led to the outcome without taking sides, leaving no stone unturned, as to what went down on that historic day. But did the council fully investigate the issue as requested by the public? NO, the special council DID NOT…

The reason as to why the special council left so many stones untouched still remains a mystery to be answered. Surely enough, the council turned one stone all ways possible many different times, but left all other stones virtually untouched.

The questions the public was asking were, of ALL the candidates running for the presidency in 2016, how come it was Donald Trump who ended up winning the election? Were there any irregularities, interference, and was the election free and fair for all the voters as mandated by the constitution of this country? In other words, when the public was asking why Donald Trump won the election, the same public was also asking why Hilary Clinton lost the election as well as how all the other candidates that ran for the presidency of United States of America that year end up losing to Donald Trump.

To answer this question, the special council was supposed to investigate all the candidates who had registered to run for the president of this country that year, irrespective of their party affiliation or even when they decided to pull out of run or when they lost. By doing so, the council would not be biased and could have had answers as to what happened. To the council, it was like solving a big puzzle where all pieces had to be turned around side to side and all possible ways for answers to be found.

For the special council to concentrate only on president elect Donald Trump, the investigators missed important clues and missed the point, leading to inconclusive investigation. Therefore all the special council could say was that there was no collusion leaving the public bewildered, wondering what then went wrong at that time. If conspiracy was out of the question, then how in the world could that happen in a society as civilized and with as many educated individuals, let alone vast resources, as the United States of America? There has to be a viable reason. In a society, things just don't start falling out of nowhere and one thing always leads to another. Something had to be there.

The reason as to why all were to be investigated is because when it comes to interfering with the presidential election, it's interfering with the constitution of this country at the highest order and therefore even the slightest anomaly is worth of note. In an election a candidate, for instance, may directly or indirectly influence another candidate winning or losing chances irrespective of whether the candidate in question won or not. Therefore to the special council, it was imperative to scrutinize all the candidates who were running for the presidency that year in order to find out if their presence, intentionally or unintentionally, influenced the final outcome of the election in 2016.

Most important of all is the fact that, if interfering with the elections was the number one suspect to the highly unwelcome outcome of the election in the public's view, then the public wanted to know as to who and how anyone was interfering with the people's constitution. Free and fair elections are the cornerstone, the foundation block, of democracy as inscribed in the constitution of this country and therefore interfering with the elections is equal to interfering with the constitutional order.

Hence thorough and complete investigation with an attempt to find all answers was vital because the country's overall order, the constitution, was on the line. This was supposed to be done and completed urgently because many societies were and still are attached to this society, as well as this nation, in one way or another and therefore there were very many from all walks of life watching from all corners. All trying to unravel what many considered as the greatest mystery in recent history.

The United States of America, being the pioneer of democracy and hence a model for many throughout the planet to follow, puts the country and the entire society at an awkward position, demanding necessary actions to be executed with great caution and expertise in order to protect and promote as well as propel democracy to new generations as well as to many other societies worldwide. Any anomaly with the United States of America's elections should be taken with seriousness to match so as not to confuse others following our footsteps as we are the leaders in democracy and should always be geared to lead by giving others better examples.

Therefore, the special council failed to realize the whole picture regarding interference and mainly concentrated solely on Russia's possibility of interference with the elections and not everyone else. Therefore if anyone else interfered differently with the election, they were left to walk away scot-free and got away with murder.

What the lead investigators, the special council, was supposed to do in such a situation was to evaluate everybody who was running for the election to be the president of this country in 2016 based on the constitution order…have the constitution of this country to be the ultimate guideline to determine everyone's eligibility to be elected as the president of this country first. From there the investigators would be able to find many other leads that needed to be looked at based on many other laws that are attached to the constitution of this country. Why you use the constitution as the only tool to start the investigation is because if the presidential position is in question, then you are dealing with the order of the land at the highest level. So as not to be biased, you need to investigate all and it's only the constitution of the country that covers all.

That is what was never done and that is why there is still that much resentment, enmity, and unreconciled anger between many leaders of this society and within the society, as no one got what they were looking for. Anger that spirals down to the general public as all leaders are attached to the society they lead in one way or another.

For the investigators to find out that there was no way Russia alone could have influenced the presidential results of the election in 2016 does not fully answer the ultimate question which is, "Why did Donald Trump get elected as the president of the United States of America in 2016?" The findings provided by the special council however only answers issues relating to one piece of the puzzle. Now the question is, "What about the rest of the pieces?"

Why the elite investigators, as well as many in society, ended up placing all cards in one basket, Russia, as the only and only culprit to the unexpected outcome of the election is a disappointment to a society which presumably is supposed to have many intelligent and wise individuals, many who know that society is complicated and an event like what happened that year may actually be as a result of multilayered issues and influences from sources far and wide.

Maybe there was too much frustration on many people's minds that resulted with an oversight, as many in the society ended up confused as to how to proceed from there. Many leaders were bewildered and unable to deliver. The outcome of the election was a surprise to the vast majority and the leaders just freaked out. Therefore, when the possibility of Russia interfering with the elections was brought up, since Russia has been the proverbial enemy to the United States of America and its allies, everybody's mind set was transfixed on Russia and Russia alone and forgot about the possibility of how if it was not Russia, forgot any other potential possibility.

It is ironic how things work though. Just the other day when Barack Obama was the president of United States of America, the greatest question was the president's legitimacy as a citizen of the United States of America by birth. Therefore, when Senator Ted Cruz from Texas was running for the presidency of the United States of America at the same time Donald Trump was running in 2016, knowing for sure that the senator was born in Calgary, Canada and migrated to United States of America when he was four years old, was the Senator not interfering with the election and hence the constitution of the United States of America? Did the senator know that Canada is another country with its own constitution and definitely not part of the United States of America? On what basis then was the senator allowed to run for the big office? Secondly, who is the registrar general who allowed the senator to run for the head principal's office of this country knowing for sure that Article 2, Section 1 of the United States of America Constitution clearly states that only those who are natural-born citizens may serve as the president of the United States of America?

This is because both Senator Ted Cruz and whoever registered the senator to run for the presidency of this country in 2016 were just playing with poor people's minds as if the poor and the weak in the society are all irrelevant and useless just because they don't know. Grandma said that just because you have it does not mean you should use it. It's always important to learn how to respect all, for all is all there is in my grandma's society. Just because many might not know all the facts does not mean that you should be taking advantage of any one. There is always the difference between those who know and those who don't. Grandma said that it is upon for those who know to teach those who don't and teach them all well and with passion, for it's always good for the society to be informed.

If, for instance, Ted Cruz had no idea about the laws of this country, even if he tried to run for the office of the president, he could have been doing so very innocently. However, the senator had been an attorney of law in the United States of America and hence knows the constitutional laws of this country off-hand. An attorney when it comes to the law of the land can never be at the same level as any other ordinary citizen of this country. The attorney's specialty is the law and should be there to be teaching others regarding what the law says and not attempting to break the same law.

Surprisingly, no one seemed to be bothered by that issue at all. None of the news agencies, reporters, newspapers, companies, not even the lawmakers in Congress and Senate, Democrats and Republicans alike, were worried about that at all. What everyone was talking about was

Russia and Russia alone. It is as if society allows a few select ones to break or attempt to break the law with no consequences or as if there are various levels of going against the constitution of this country. How if it was the senator who won the Republican ticket that year rather than Donald Trump? What could have happened? No wonder Heaven favored Donald Trump to be the president during that period of time.

Saying that Russia was doing more harm to the society of the United States of America than the senator is equivalent to saying that someone stands a better chance in hitting a target located miles away on a foggy rainy midnight with a blunt spear as compared to someone else shooting at point blank range on a sunny calm midday with a laser-guided hand-gun. Interference multiplied by interference equals interference and when it comes to the constitution of the country, there should be no favoritism for that is the LAW and the law is blind and should be left that way with no surgical interventions necessary for a better, safer, and prosperous tomorrow.

What is so interesting about the society of today is how everyone takes anything literally or for granted. There needs to be some seriousness in some matters as this society, as much you might love it, might end up in the drain just like your predecessors did just a few years ago.

Jesus told you just the other day that you seem to be worried so much about minute dusting on the outside of the cup, not knowing that it is the lethal poison on the inside of the same cup that might kill you. My grandma speaks Swahili. Grandma said, "Kikulacho kinguoni mwako." The bug that might bite you the best is the one hiding on your inner clothes.

The governing bodies of the society were supposed to realize that there was a problem, an unusual occurrence, an unexpected outcome, and then investigate in order to analyze the extent of the problem and how the problem can affect the entire society before placing measures with an attempt to overcome the issue. Failure to realize and accept that the problem exists is the greatest mistake any leader can ever make because that channels the society to walk in the dark, blindly making unnecessary and unwanted changes that might end up hurting the society even more. Investigation is never meant to change the results or the outcome. Investigation is done in order to gather data or information necessary regarding what happened. It is always better to know as well as be informed for an informed society always makes better and more viable decisions for the future.

It is impossible to change history. Whatever happened has already happened. It's a done-deal and the day is too far gone. You can only be looking forward to a better tomorrow. Therefore you investigate with the intent to gain enough knowledge related to the issue at hand that happened in the society so that if it is bad, you can prevent it from happening tomorrow. Never investigate any issue within the society with an intent to change history, for history is irreversible. Always investigate with the intent to stop continuation of bad or unwanted history. For history has a very strong and powerful reputation of repeating itself.

If you don't fully and thoroughly investigate the problem, then you won't know what happened and up to what extent the society was affected. Therefore you won't be able to find the truth, the light, and will be walking blind in virtual darkness not knowing how, when, and where to turn and in which direction.

While the investigation was ongoing, the government matters were supposed to proceed unperturbed as if nothing was going on until the final revelation was revealed as to what happened, the parties involved, and to what extent the damage was done. The knowledge and information gathered would help allow society to adjust and re-adjust as necessary to cater changes, if any.

Therefore for Congress and Senate to reject the president just because the president did not have the political inner circle expertise, was a newcomer to Washington, and was definitely not someone to push around, the lawmakers ends up failing because Donald Trump never elected himself to office. Rather it is the public of United States of America that elected him. You fail for not giving the president a chance and all the support deemed possible so that if the president fails to accomplish the job, the same public that elected Donald Trump to office will be the same public that sends the president back home.

Today, the country is in turmoil with never-ending war between the president and the Congress, the battle to figure out who is who, thereby leaving public issues unattended. It is a war between two very strong bulls with none ready to give in. Hence it's the grass, the poor in society, that suffers. Both parties need to come to realization that the public needs them both and that is why they both are elected by the public to be there and learn how to keep their differences aside and work together. That is what they both are mandated to do by the public that elected them to power and also by the constitution of this country.

If only the special council could have conducted full all-around investigation, the council could have found out that there were a few interfering with the people of the United States of America's business and not just Russia. But the president was favored by the constitution and therefore it is the constitution of the United States of America that dictated the terms because at the end of the long and tedious day, candidate Donald Trump was constitutionally on the right and candidate Hilary Clinton was unconstitutional. In very simple words, what happened during that election year in 2016 was that at the end of the day, everyone else had lost and the race had only two major contenders remaining: Donald Trump and Hilary Clinton. One contender was disqualified and thereby remained with only one contender as the ultimate finalist and just like that, Donald Trump became the president of the United States of America. That is why even Donald Trump could tell that a miracle must have happened because that win was truly against ALL ODDS.

It could have been too costly for the public to repeat the election process and even super costly to the entire society if the constitutional order was broken. Therefore in the end, the public just ended up with another leader. A different leader than the one everyone seemed to be accustomed to. That is why it's taking so long for society to re-adjust and leaders to accept the reality, if any will ever find that necessary.

If this was a test that Heaven provided to the people of United States of America with the intent to find out whether the society is mature enough to conquer the future and easily adjust to changing times, society, and leadership, everyone probably FAILED and failed terribly because everyone seems to just be concerned about themselves and their immediate issues and fails to realize what was and still is at stake. Russia or any other society could only have interfered with the 2016 elections indirectly for the most part, as they all know their limits and extent before closing the thin line. It is the direct interference that always hit the society the most, let you all be informed.

Jesus told you that you seem to be more interested with a few gold coins you can see with your near-blind eyes and easily forget the vast riches that await ahead. There are times to sit down and think and before you start thinking, you think again. For the wise man said, "Not everything that shines is GOLD," and "Looks can be deceiving," Grandma said. It is always better to look forward for a better future while moving with great caution armed with a lot of passion while being guided by wisdom for the winding road is very tricky, rough, slippery, and full of many enemies scouting from all sides.

The main issue regarding this election that bothers many in this country as well as the world at large is why and how did Donald Trump end up winning the election? The answer to that question is complicated as the main question should be why did Hilary Clinton lose the election to Donald Trump?

Why did Hilary Clinton lose the presidential election 2016?

It was because Hilary Clinton was one hundred percent unconstitutional from Heaven's point of view and also one hundred percent unconstitutional based on the constitution of the United States of America's standpoint.

How Hilary was unconstitutional based on Heaven?

Heaven holds the constitution of any country or society with BOTH HANDS. Hence the constitution of this country is always in good hands, at least for the sake of the poor and the weak, many who without help would end up being misused, abused, and neglected by the few rich and powerful in the society. It is the Bible that says, "Then shall no one separate those two who are meant to be together," and therefore Heaven considers Hilary and Bill Clinton as one unit and not two separate entities.

Hence, as far as heaven is concerned, if one of the two was the president of the United States of America before, the other one was also the president as both are considered as one soul and one body by heaven. Therefore since Hilary's husband Bill Clinton had been the president of United States of America before for two straight terms, Hilary Clinton was also the president. She shared the same duties that go with that position with Bill Clinton at the same time. Therefore Hilary Clinton was not to be allowed to be the president of this country again as the constitution prohibited Bill Clinton from going back to that office for another term.

More so, it is also written in the Bible that the wife was created to be the helper of the husband. Therefore if Hilary Clinton was to be the president of this country, Bill Clinton was also to be part and parcel of the deal. What Hilary was doing as a great wife was to hand over her beloved husband a perfect present, the presidency of the country, for it was the husband, Bill Clinton, who was to be regarded as the president of this country by Heaven and not Hilary Clinton, as many might think. If you don't believe it, then you need to go and read your Bible very well.

More so, there are many in the society who were supporting Hilary Clinton on her venture as the first female president of this country with the hope that Bill Clinton, having valuable expertise, would be there to help Hilary, not knowing that the constitution of the United States of America prohibits Bill Clinton from being in that office for another term or two.

Therefore Hilary Clinton did not get elected as the president of United States of America because of being a woman, as many might tend to think or believe. Rather because Hilary Clinton and Bill Clinton had been in that office before and hence were both barred by the constitution of this country from being in that same office again for the rest of their lives.

That does not mean that Bill Clinton and Hilary Clinton are anywhere near being bad people, both might probably be some of the best people you can ever meet, but the constitution of the United States of America doesn't and should never choose sides because it is the law and the law is BLIND.

It is a hard pill to swallow though, for no one likes to fail however it is the truth. If for instance Bill Clinton had never been in office before, Hilary Clinton could probably have won the election and become the president of this country today, at least in the eyes of the people, while Bill Clinton was to be the one dealing with complicated issues in office regarding the public and the society at large.

Many people have tendency to take things and issues for granted, there are some aspects of nature that never changes and any time anyone tries to change that, bad things happen. It is always better to remember that all are important. However the neck can never surpass the head and therefore you should never think that just because it is the wife who got elected that the husband wasn't and vice versa. Both are one unit and not two separate entities in the eyes of the Lord.

Why was Hilary Clinton unconstitutional based on the constitution of the United States of America?

It was desperate to many that their favorite candidate didn't make it that day and I truly feel bad for them all, for many didn't know much and the few who knew the facts were too ignorant to inform the public about the truth. The fact is the president of the United States of America can only be someone who has never been in office before and can only be elected for two terms in their life time. Therefore, as much as many in the country and around the world at large supported Hilary Clinton as history in the making, for Hilary was to be the first female president the country has ever seen, and as great as the United States of America's government was when Bill Clinton was in office, Bill Clinton could only be in that office for a maximum of two terms. Since Bill Clinton had been through that, any attempt to get back into that office again was and still is against the law of the land and that's what the constitution of the United States of America says.

In all due respect, this country was actually in good hands when Bill Clinton was the president of the United States of America. Hence many viewed that if Hilary could be the next president, Bill Clinton would be there to offer a helping hand and therefore the good old times would be back for the better of all in the nation as well as many abroad who cherish the United States of America's ideas and way of life. However, the constitution of the United States of America could not allow direct contributions of Bill Clinton in government matters for another term. That's why no matter how well things would have been with Hilary as the president of United States of America, that could not materialize because the law clearly says "NO" in CAPITAL letters.

This is because, for instance, if Hilary Clinton was to the president of the United States of America, was there any probability that former president Bill Clinton, being her husband, could have stayed out of government matters at all costs? Not a chance, because it is in nature that the husband helps the wife anytime things get tough. Remember, it is written in the Bible that the wife is the helper. Therefore if Hilary was to be the president, her and Bill Clinton were both to be working together as one unit at the same house they are so familiar with as they were already there twice before, a place they both knew all the corners and crevices and probably required little to no orientation. Hence it was and still is unconstitutional because to the public, electing Hilary was equivalent to electing BILL for the third term in office.

Furthermore, where was Bill Clinton to live? Probably in the same White House the former president owned and operated for two terms straight and therefore was to be there against the constitution of this country if Hilary Clinton was elected. This is because for Bill Clinton, being the husband of Hilary Clinton and therefore the head of the household, It would have been Bill Clinton to be calling out all the shots again against the law of the land because the former presidents tenure in office was over and done with as far as the constitution of this country is concerned.

The president of United States of America is there to serve the people and therefore while in office is provided a permanent living quarters by the public, the White House. That house is government property and hence the public can only pay the rent and all the bills for the president of the United States of America for only two terms and not three or four times because that's what the constitution says. Has anyone heard of any president being asked for gas and electric bill while in office? If not, how did anyone expect for Bill Clinton's family to have their bills payed off by the public for the third time against the order of the land?

What people need to understand is that the president of the United States of America is not a title but a duty that comes with that position, the right to serve the people of United States of America with undivided attention. That is why among all three government top DOGS: legislative, judicial and executive, it is only the executive side that by the constitution requires its head to be in office for a maximum of two terms in order to give many other leaders nationwide the same opportunity to lead the country.

Therefore Hilary Clinton did not lose the election because of being a woman, because was incapable of leading the country, or even because Hilary is a bad person, BUT because Hilary Clinton was there before in the same office twice. Therefore for Hilary to be back in that same office again was against the constitution of the United States of America.

By the way, Donald Trump asked Hilary Clinton a few times during the presidential campaign in 2016 as to what Hilary was eager to finish that never got finished when both Bill and Hilary Clinton were in office for two terms before. Also Donald Trump told the public on several occasions that Hilary Clinton was unconstitutional and should not be allowed to run for the president of the United States of America. However, hardly anyone was listening to Donald Trump, let alone contemplating what that might mean, because many in the society were transfixed with the notion of Hilary making history as the first female president of United States of America. Nothing else mattered in many people's minds other than that, only to end up with a different kind of history in the making, their worst nightmare.

If Hilary was not to be the president, then why Donald Trump?

Because among all the other candidates it was only Donald Trump who was telling the public the truth regarding Hilary Clinton being disqualified by the constitution and hence ended up being favored by heaven. As you all know, NO ONE LOVES THE TRUTH BETTER THAN HEAVEN. That's why Donald Trump ended up facing Hilary Clinton in the finals leading the society to have no other choice other than Donald Trump, as Hilary Clinton had already been rejected by the constitution from being the president of United States of America for another term. That was why no matter how many blunders Donald Trump seemed to make, no matter how many individuals candidate Trump attacked, no matter how much Donald Trump was deemed to be a looser by many through all political predictions and polls and no matter how many multi-layered scandals seemed to tail the candidate, Donald Trump ended up being elected as the president of United States of America against all odds. It was as if the public had already made up its mind even before the election started.

The society needs to know that there are different kinds of leaders: leaders in business, in farming, in engineering and so on. At the same time there are leaders of society popularly known as true leaders. None of the candidates from any parties running for the president of the United States of America at that time was a true leader of the society because the only one who was very close to a true leader was Bill Clinton through Hilary Clinton.

Who is a true leader? A true leader is a philosopher, someone who believes with the society, someone who no matter how rich or how much money the individual might possess believes in better working of the society and hence would always try better means to aid the society in an attempt for the people the leader rules to reach higher standards of life. To a philosopher, the real riches lie in the people's hands and not on the leader's. The leader feels better or rich when many in the society are capable of meeting their needs with ease.

When the electorate were presented by the choices of the potential future president, the decision was mainly based on who among them all was the better choice, one who could better push the country forward for a better tomorrow, for the day was already too far gone. This is because the society could still comfortably be led by any leader no matter the leader's specialty as long as the leader is able to work with other leaders at various levels of the government in order to meet the needs of the society. For instance the elected leader can even be an engineer or a farmer who knows very little about the society's working. But by having other leaders of the society around that chosen leader, the society runs very efficiently. Therefore anyone can be elected as the president as it all depends on the circumstances at hand. More so the constitution does not discriminate anyone from becoming the overall head of the society in United States of America as long as the candidate is within the set up guidelines outlined by the constitution of this country.

What happened was that the public of United States of America and their many well-wishers ended up with a different kind of a leader that the society was not accustomed to and hence everyone freaked out. First of all, the vast majority of the world's population, let alone very many within the United States of America, never expected President Donald Trump to win and many were already very busy preparing to welcome the first female president of United States of America. But they didn't know what heaven had in store for them, the shock of their lives. The society has tendency to forget too quickly as it was just the other day when a wise man said that even if the crop in the field looks very healthy and mature, that does not mean it's time to widen the granary. Things can change faster than a flip of a switch.

Many in the leadership's inner circle were wondering as to how they were to work with the newcomer who had little to no knowledge about how business in Washington runs, had little experience in the political arena, and someone who during the campaign trail had just informed everyone in a language all could understand that the new president was not someone to push around and was not also to listen to anyone not unless they were listening to the president too. Someone who is there to run things in a completely different style unknown to anyone in the Washington political arena.

Hence the leaders forgot that all they had to do was to accept their responsibility as leaders too and learn how to work with one another. It is the Almighty who sent us all here to the planet to work with one another and hence in any situation we should learn how to leave our differences behind and work together for a better society. You don't have to love the president for you to work with the president! If it is your duty then it is and hence leaders should perform their job with unconditional attitude for the sake of the poor in the society and also for the country they all love.

During the campaign to determine as to who was to represent each party, everyone who was running on both sides, including the independent candidates, were all informed about several issues facing the country. One was the war and the other was their constitution and the future of the society of the United States of America.

The main reason was that when The United States of America's society was formulated many years ago, the majority of the population was immigrants from many regions of the world who had varying cultural beliefs and ways of life. As years passed, the population of those born in the United States of America naturally started to increase and hence with the generational change, there is always the need for the society to readjust to the changing times and needs in order to meet the new generation's needs and demands.

Therefore, there has been severe friction between the interests of the new generation of those belonging to United States of America by birth, many who feel that their issues should be handled first at all cost, and the older generation that realizes that it is the presence of immigrants in this country that has helped the country to prosper at that fast pace and therefore immigrants should not be ignored. These are two schools of thought that naturally exist within the society of United States of America and each has its own legitimate basis. It is always the job of the leaders, and especially the lawmakers in Congress and in the Senate, to make relevant adjustments of the law so as to meet the demands of the society as time go by.

The constitution of this country was formulated with the vision of what might happen later on when the mainstream society changes such that the majority switch from being immigrants to individuals born in this country. That is why per the constitution, the president since he is the overall head of the society, must always be someone born in the country and thereby start preparing the society early for the predicted transition that was bound to happen later by safeguarding the interests and needs of many born in the country. The main aim of the constitution is to have a smooth transition within the society with the goal for the United States of America to finally emerge from being dependent on immigrants to heavily being dependent on their own home-grown boys and girls slowly with the passage of time.

This issue was a carefully crafted thought and most likely was based on how many rich and influential individuals from other places and other societies were getting interested with the newly-found land and they were taking over the country like a swarm. The forefathers may have feared that whoever might end up being born later on in the United States of America stood a possibility of being out-manipulated and abused by the rich whose only interest was to get even richer at the expense of the poor if nothing was done and done early.

Therefore in order to formulate the law of the land in favor of the population born in the United States of America, the forefathers guaranteed that the absolute head of the society of the United States of America shall always be someone born in this country and can only be there for a maximum of two terms such that even if whoever the president is gets manipulated by the rich, that can only happen for a very short period of time because when the next president is sworn in to power things change to another direction.

However, it's important to understand that for the country to survive at present pace its population of the in-born (those born in the United States of America) has to be over seventy-five percent, over two-thirds of the working adults directly involved in the function of the society and the government one way or another, while the rest of the population comprises of citizens by naturalization, immigrants, and visitors. Most likely the United States of America's society may have already reached that level or is very close thereby demanding some re-adjustments to be made in a hurry in order to cater to the changing times and the changing society. This may be what led the society to demand for a different kind of a leader as the society may be getting tired of dealing with the same leaders who are just there and not addressing the changing society's needs.

Anytime the society ever gets faced with such unusual and unexpected outcomes, there has to be something else going on within the society that needs to be addressed urgently. Whatever is happening serves as a message to all in the United States of America and their many well-wishers, a message that not everything is in good shape, and hence allows the society to re-evaluate itself. For Grandma said, "If you can't find out what is eating you that's from a distance, you need to stop and re-evaluate yourself and your immediate surroundings for you may be the problem and you might not even know it."

Nevertheless during the campaign in 2016, many of the candidates went to the war issue, each laying down plans as how to better handle the war if they ever got elected but none other than Donald Trump ever tried to address the immigration issue by talking about the wall. Notably the society of the United States of America has been dealing with immigration issues for quite some time and maybe a separation of some kind sounded like a viable starting point to many.

Donald Trump therefore ended up being the favorite from heaven's stand point because the president was telling the truth at all costs with little concern whether he was to win or not, while the constitution disqualified Hilary Clinton leaving the public with no other choice. The rest of the candidates may have had information regarding Hilary being unconstitutional but may not have known as to how and therefore opted not to talk about it with concerns about how that might affect their interpersonal relationship in their political careers. But Donald Trump didn't care and said it all in broad daylight when everyone was listening.

Since heaven believes that if you can tell the truth today then you are capable of telling the truth tomorrow, Donald Trump became the better choice for the society as the next president. When it reached the finals, Hilary versus Trump, it was either Donald Trump or no one as Hilary Clinton was automatically disqualified and that was all it took, which meant that it was either Donald Trump as the president of the United States of America or the entire election process had to be repeated once more because the constitution could not allow Hilary Clinton to win the election.

This is because there is no way you can tell Heaven that the president is supposed to be in office only twice and then come around trying to impose someone else to be in office for the third time and still expect

Heaven to drop on its knees for you! That has never happened before and definitely wasn't to start happening then. If, however, the society in the United States of America demanded for Hilary Clinton to win the election, all the lawmakers had to do was amend the constitution so that anyone who might end up in such a predicament to be allowed back in the big office in the future.

For the President Donald Trump, just like any other candidate who was running for the president of the United States of America in 2016, is a leader but a leader in entertainment. Furthermore, who was the leader of Celebrity Apprentice among other entertainment businesses across the society just before the 2016 election? Donald Trump. Everyone who was running for the presidency at that time is a leader in varying fields of leadership and it ended up being Donald Trump, the entertainer, triumphant over the rest and hence became the president of the United States of America. That explains as to why when the president was inaugurated, the new president's chosen commentator told everyone that, "That was greatest inauguration ceremony ever PERIOD."

What the public doesn't understand is how to differentiate between each individual's leadership styles. For an entertainer, everything the leader does has to be "very good," "the best," or "the greatest" because that is how their soul was created by the Almighty to act and live. Since there is no way you can question the Almighty in creating anyone the way they are, all we can learn is how to live and accommodate one another. For instance, to many in the society, the president is a proverbial liar because people view the president as not telling the truth as they know it. Whilst what the society needs to know is that to an entertainer, telling a story in order to get the job done is warranted to some extent. For instance, it is okay for the newly-elected President Donald Trump, being naturally a leader in entertainment, to claim that the president got elected by the largest Electoral College, had the most peaceful inauguration ever, and even had the largest crowd than any of the leader's predecessors ever had during their inauguration! While in reality the actual facts speak to something else completely different and the numbers don't even add up, let alone agree.

This is because the leader is living the dream come true at that specific moment. Hence, as a leader in entertainment and especially after winning the highest prize in the entire society, everything had to be the best and greatest possible ever PERIOD. However it is not allowed for anyone to tell a lie that might end up jeopardizing someone else life. People need to learn how to make the distinction between the two, distinguish the difference between telling a story from telling a lie. Therefore whenever you talk about someone either telling the truth or not, just try to think about the intent and also who that might be because you might not know whether it's a story or a lie.

The president, even if he is a leader in entertainment, is a leader with capability to see the country move forward if given a chance. However that seems like a very long shot for Donald Trump as the president is facing the toughest rejection than any other president before him ever faced while in office. What the society and especially the public in the United States of America don't know is that the more the resistance, the more the confusion, and the more nothing gets done. The president, no matter what kind of leadership the leader uses, is an individual and hence incapable of running the government single-handedly. Therefore he requires a helping hand from all other leaders across the nation in order to serve the people of the United States of America and the world at large satisfactorily. That is why there is the Congress, the Senate, and the Judiciary among other leaders there to aid the president. If the country fails for instance, it is not just the president who fails. Rather the blame goes to all parties involved.

Let me ask you, even if you decide to remove the president from office today, who is there to claim that Donald Trump never became the forty-fifth president of the United States of America? NO ONE. History has already been made. Everyone seems to be very confused about what is going on and hence might end up looking for a repetition of history if not worse. The society need to understand that the United States of America is not personal property of the president. The country belongs to all that live here as well as many with a close association to this country. Hence, if there is anyone the public has elected to represent them in office, may it be in congress or the senate and even the president, all should be held accountable for their failures to serve the people as they were all elected to do and not just the president alone.

The country is failing terribly not because Donald Trump is not doing what the president is supposed to do, but because the other leaders who the public elected to get the job done all decide to sit down and have a great time. It is as if there is a silent standoff between other elected officials and the president, a standoff between the constitution of this country and the current government leaders.

It is evident that both Congress and Senate were not prepared to work with the president since day one as both parties viewed the new leader as unfit, unqualified, and hence unwelcome and therefore wanted the leader out of office at all costs. If the president was elected by the public to do the job, why the rejection by other leaders, the lawmakers? This might make you wonder, does anyone in this country expect themselves to be more important than the society itself? More superior than the constitution of this country?

Everyone in the political arena knew and still knows that the president did not have the Washington political inner circle connection or the expertise and hence required a helping hand just to get through the narrow aisles, let alone make a few turns around the block. The majority of the leaders expected the president to fail as to many of them Donald Trump was unwelcome at the dinner table because none of them expected Trump to win the election in the first place. Therefore the only game was to push the newly-elected leader left and right until the president gives up and leave the office. That is yet to happen as Donald Trump has already proven to them all that the president isn't the best choice to fight with.

Whenever the president suggested someone to fill his failing cabinet and the Congress together with the Senate don't agree to the choices made, has any one of them, either the Republicans or the Democrats, ever suggested a list of several candidates for the president to choose from such that now the president has more choices? Absolutely not! Because all you are accustomed to is to criticize and blame the president rather than get the job done as your constituents asked you to do. Hardly anyone is concerned about the poor anguishing on the streets as to many of the leaders, going against the presidents proposals, ideas, or even what the president is talking about seems to be of more importance than even helping the society and hence the country succeed.

This is mainly so because many in Washington political inner circle only know how to criticize their opponent using traditional politics and since Donald Trump tends to run things as if independent of any party, both parties Republicans and Democrats feels left out. Therefore they are only interested to see the president fail rather than help the country and the society they both love. Many leaders from either side, whether in the Congress or in the Senate, have spent valuable time trying to see and weigh in on possible modalities to have the president kicked out of office. Instead of spending time on issues that bother the society the most, many are only interested in talking about what President Donald Trump is doing or not doing.

Many of the leaders in Washington were really disappointed that the special council they founded and supported found no wrongdoing between the Russian government and the president-elect Donald Trump during the campaign trail in 2016. Therefore the only possible reason to legally put the president off office was out of the question and many were now banking on the issue of obstruction of justice as the last option because none of the lawmakers are ready to give in and accept the reality.

If and only if the lawmakers were considering possibility of obstruction of justice based on the fact that president Donald Trump fired former director of FBI James Comey soon after the director of FBI initiated the investigation relating to Russia illegally interfering with the 2016 elections, the lawmakers had a viable argument to make and a potential possibility it could go through until the former FBI director told everyone who was listening that the director did not trust the president at all and that the mistrust had reached to a point where the former director was secretly writing sticky notes any time the director discussed issues with the president.

For the government to run effectively there needs to be trust between the president and the director of FBI because FBI is extremely important branch of Homeland Security. Therefore if the head of FBI and the commander-in-chief do not trust one another, one of them has to leave and since the president is the overall boss of the entire department of Homeland Security, then the former director of FBI had to leave office so that the president can find someone else who can trust him and hence work with the president for the public of the United States of America and the required services provided by the FBI, irrespective of who's the head are extremely important. More so if the former director of FBI did not trust the new commander-in-chief, the entire FBI would not be on good terms with the president. Hence it was better for another director who was ready to work with the new president to step in. Therefore the president made a great judgment in firing James Comey as there has to be trust between the president and all other leaders working around the president, the FBI director being one of them, for the government to run efficiently.

What many need to understand is that society is beyond the individual. It might sound harsh or unfair for the former director to have been fired, but the president has the entire society to run and therefore when asking for complete trust, it's in relation on how to conduct business under the president as mandated by the constitution.

The major problem was that many of the leaders believed and still believe that President Donald Trump got into office dishonestly. Hence there were many not ready to work with the new president as they viewed that the president was to be in office for a very short period of time before being found guilty and get kicked out by the law.

Many may argue that the president was forcing the former director to do what the director felt was out of the way or even that the president fired the former director for initiating the investigation against the president, but all that holds no water because it was James Comey who openly said to everyone that the former director of FBI did not trust the new president, thereby giving the president no choice other than to fire him.

The worst mistake the former director made was to openly disclose information that should have been kept silent because by telling the public about that mistrust and of that high of a level, just gives absolute justification for the commander-in-chief to have let the director go as he was not trustworthy to the president. Therefore he was not capable of running the FBI effectively while under president Donald Trump.

James Comey probably forgot that Grandma said that we should never fight with anger because whenever you start fighting with anger you end up fighting blind. You end up fighting with the wrong one as well as lose control of the situation. As Grandma said, "It pays to go to war armed with intelligence, with a lot of passion for the society, while guided by wisdom and not by anger."

The director of FBI is the head of all investigators, the chief investigator general, and therefore should be the very last individual to disclose any information on the director's hands. Therefore for the former director of FBI to publicly say that he distrusted the president and was secretly writing notes soon after meeting with the president Trump clearly shows that the level of mistrust as well as the dislike the former director of FBI had for President Donald Trump was at the highest level. The two leaders were incapable to see one another eye to eye. Incapable of working together in unity in leading the country as well as the society and hence left the commander-in-chief with no other choice but to replace the chief of investigators with another chief for the society had to keep on moving no matter what the circumstances. If, however, the former director got fired and kept quiet, it could have been argued that there were other reasons relating to that firing.

That disclosure by James Comey, as innocent as might sound, only heightened the worries of the general public because of the trust the public has for the FBI and hence contributed to more confusion among the people. Many people trust the FBI and therefore if the head of the FBI was so scared of the president as to be writing notes after the meetings with new commander-in-chief, to the public, the president then has to be a monster not fit to be in office. The reality is that it was lapse in judgment on the director's side for moving too fast in disclosing any information rather than waiting and gathering all evidence before making any moves in order to avoid making wrong approach to the problem. Of course not, unless the former director of FBI was taking that opportunity to build his own personal political future with the public trust and concerns at bay.

The FBI is property of the United States government and operates independently of any political influence, has no religious affiliation, and goes across the board of all walks of life and traditions within this country. Like the law, the chief leader in all investigations in this country, the FBI, is supposed to be blind, dealing with issues of law as they are irrespective of the odds, if any. Therefore this department is entrusted by all in the nation and holds many secrets relating to many peoples' lives within the country for the sake of their security. None of those secrets are supposed to be in jeopardy while in the hands of the FBI. Therefore all members of the FBI are supposed to seal the information on their hands carefully, learn how to keep secrets, and also learn how to safely disclose the information to other government entities so as to prevent confusion within the society. The leaders of this crucial department of the United States government should be the very last individuals to disclose any information to the general public freely and should always weigh in with great caution and seriousness to match on how any information released to the general public might affect the society and to what extent. Whenever there is a problem in the society requiring the FBI intervention, the information gathered and how to conduct the investigation should only be shared by the responsible parties and not the general public not unless that was the intent to start with.

For the former director of FBI to publicly disclose his distrust and dislike of the president elect freely to the public at that time was a little bit reckless on the side of James Comey because that just raised the temperature on the public, and it was already over 110 degrees. It added more fuel to the blazing fire. The former leader of FBI by doing so allowed his own personal ego, interests, and wishes to overcome the leader's obligation to serve the public of the United States of America, independent of any influence while operating at a neutral zone. It was this disclosure that amplified the confusion within the society over what had just happened during the election.

The leader of the FBI should never be the first to disclose the information because that may affect the overall trust general public has for the entire FBI. As a leader, there are some things and issues that you should learn how to keep quiet and silent about. Learn to accept that not everything is meant to go your way, learn how to accept, and receive a few bumps and bruises at least for the sake of the society you serve.

For James Comey to disclose that information to the public, the director of FBI being the boss of all investigators that work in and on secretes and instead of doing his duty of advising the newly elected president of the United States of America on how to best keep all information discussed in the White House from leaking to the public, James Comey ended up willingly and purposely leaking important white house information to the public in person. This proved that the director was not ready to work with the newly elected president and had already made up his mind. Therefore the president had absolutely no other choice other than to let the director go in order to open the door for a new director who would be ready to work with the president.

Donald Trump was just asking James Comey as the director of FBI for complete loyalty mainly because the president-elect found the head of FBI there in office. Hence he did not nominate the director. More so many leaders like Donald Trump prefer to give other leaders under them complete autonomy of the job such that the leader runs the assigned branch independently of the president and relate to the president as if the president is equal to that specific leader. In such a case, the president would require complete loyalty from that leader. Complete loyalty just means that both of you as leaders are leading society as one unit and everyone has total responsibility of whatever one is assigned to. In other words, how the government works under leaders like Donald Trump is that all leaders under the president work together as a panel independent of the president. They only go to the president if they need more help and even then they all talk or relate to the president as if the president is their equal leader.

It is the higher end government in a democratic society where the society is governed by many leaders all who have parallel powers and responsibilities allowing power to be shared by many leaders equally all under one roof, the president, rather than having the president elect being the only one holding all the power. That is how civilized democratic governments work or are supposed to work. That is what Donald Trump was expecting when the president got elected and started talking about making America better again and so on, but instead was handed total rejection from other leaders the president was to work with for unknown reasons, all fighting with anger and not knowing that if you fight with anger you lose and therefore all ended up fighting an already lost war.

However because former director of FBI, just like any other leader in Washington, was already prepared to work with Hilary Clinton and not

Donald Trump, James Comey took that query from the president as an offense and went to war with the president thereby dragging everyone else with him up to this day. He decided to fight with anger and therefore lost the war for Donald Trump is a worrier who won't mind going after you the dirtiest way possible.

It is always important for those who are entrusted by the public not to be misleading and confusing many in the society because a confused society is incapable of moving forward easily. The conflict between the leaders never does the society any good and only adds more resentment and anger upon those they serve thereby weakening unity among many in the society.

The ones that suffering the most are many poor souls who heavily depend on the United States of America for guidance as a leader of the modern world. Many who were waiting for promised answer to the results of the elections they never saw coming in 2016 only to be told that nothing out of the ordinary happened, while even themselves can smell of something happening because of the animosity depicted by leaders against one another in this country. What the leaders of this nation need to understand is that the confusion in the society of this nation only amplifies our weakness to the enemy, for the enemy is watching who is fighting who and for what. Not everybody likes or loves you and just as there are very many who love you, there are quite a handful who won't mind celebrating your downfall.

Grandma advised leaders to lead wisely and, while leading, to always place the concerns and needs of those to be led first before theirs. Today it is the opposite, the one to be led are all irrelevant as the leaders are more concerned about who matters the most or who is who among themselves leaving the society to keep waiting for their service with no avail.

However, irrespective of the worries and confusion that's dominating Washington today, the lawmakers still need to understand that there are laws to be made in this country for the society has to survive regardless of who won the election or who lost, regardless of who is who. Therefore when the president is leading the country, the lawmakers should also be doing their job because adjusting the laws governing the society in this country is the main job of the lawmakers and will always remain their main agenda as that is what they are all elected by the public to do. Per the constitution of the United States of America it is the Congress that has the power to make laws that govern the country and not the president. All laws start as a bill that passes through Congress first before heading to the Senate to be scrutinized by the elite in the political world and after that the president signs the bill into law. All the president has is the power to make executive orders, which are supposed to be for emergency cases, while waiting for Congress to make the lasting changes of the law.

Therefore if there is a problem in the society like there is regarding immigrants popping across the border ready to step in at all costs, who is supposed to address the issue? Congress and the Senate. Is there anyone out there among them who is ready, let alone willing, to tackle the issue? Absolutely none. Why? Because they all know very well that immigration issues are always a hot mess and no one is ready to get their sparkling clean hands dirty. Therefore, they left the president to deal with the issue single-handedly. Today all you hear is how much the president has failed in handling the issue while none of them lawmakers of the land are there to give a helping hand by adjusting the law in order to deal with the problem.

The Congress and Senate are there to make necessary adjustments to the law in order to cater for the ever-changing society and while doing so, project for the future society's needs. Today, everyone is doing whatever they want, making laws that doesn't even make any sense as far as the future of the society of the United States of America is concerned, leaving behind what the society urgently need to be done untouched.

An issue like immigration can not be left on the hands of only one in-dividual, the president, in a society full of many leaders like there are in the United States of America and still expect everything to sail smoothly. The necessary adjustments require multilayered panels of leaders, from religious leaders to many other leaders, from the grassroots of the entire society to participate, all working with passion for a better future society while guided by wisdom and not by hatred between one another, let alone the entire forefront of all top leaders in the Congress, the Senate, judicial system, and also the president for the issues of immigrations in this country to finally get resolved. This process can only be initiated by Congress but instead of doing so, they are all busy fighting over whether the public had the right to elect President Donald Trump or not.

It is not the President Donald Trump failing the country today as we speak, rather the Congress and the Senate combined, both Democrats and the Republicans alike. This is because the main job of the president is to make sure that the country's population is well–fed and that there is no regress in the society from the time the president takes office and there is progress in people's lives and their well-being. This is because not everybody can fit in White House in one sitting for breakfast or dinner every day. Hence, making sure that everyone has food on the table, wherever that table might be in the country, is the main and should be the main priority of any leader and so far President Trump has not failed in doing that.

It is the Congress and the Senate that is supposed to make sure that all other issues are taken care of. The president has enough supporting help in the cabinet and in the White House and they also aid the president in making sure that the country is safe as well as inform the president as to which areas might need immediate attention and which can wait for a minute or two. It is the Congress and the Senate that ultimately decides who should and also who should not work under the president. All of the president's cabinet members have to go through the Congress and the Senate before final approval for their job. Therefore, for the government to work effectively, all the lawmakers have to do is to make sure that the president's cabinet is full of able individuals who care about this country and therefore will get the assigned job done. But since the lawmakers don't like President Donald Trump, they are more concerned about Donald Trump's government succeeding and not looking at the possibility of the society failing. They are more concerned about who will take credit of the society's success while under President Donald Trump over the entire society's survival.

Just because the lawmakers dislike Donald Trump as the president of the United States of America does not mean that they should let the society down. All should come to realization and acceptance that somehow, someway the president of the United States of America is Donald J Trump, try to understand the president's leadership style, and then move from there as they all should do if it was any other president that they all are accustomed to. Just take it as a learning experience. New leadership, new challenges, new ways to get things done, and a new day to keep moving forward and not backward.

So far all you hear is all about the fight between the elected officials and the president which clearly indicates even to a layman that the country is divided and ready to fall apart and guess who will be to blame if that ever ends up happening? The elected officials, all of them, and not just the president. The most important thing for all of us is to learn how to manage our differences in order to reach for a positive outcome for our society, learn how to better manage our anger, and come to realization that just because we are not alike and don't even like one another, we all can come around and work together for a better future and for the sake of the future of the society we both value and love the most.

What most are worried about today is to why and how the election got interfered with. In reality what everyone in this country should worry about the most is how to prevent what happened in 2016 from happening again in the future. The surest way to prevent outsiders from interfering is to have an independent society and most likely that is the wall that the president keeps talking about. However with all due respects to the president, even Donald Trump may have misinterpreted that very information. What the society was asking is actually not a physical wall, but an ideological wall that would separate the society in the United States of America from everyone else and hence help to finally foster for the ultimate independence of this society. This is because as it stands today the United States of America is not an independent society because United States of America is still a nation of immigrants. Until America graduates from being dependent from immigrants, interferences from foreign societies like what happened during the previous election are guaranteed to re-occur in the future which might end up leading to deadly if not lethal repercussions to this society.

Mark the difference between the two carefully. An independent country is a country that can make its own laws independent of any other nation and whose population is adequate to meet the needs of those living in that society. The United States of America is an independent country, but its population has been struggling to meet the demands of the society itself and therefore have been forced to turn in to migrants in order to balance the equation. But as time goes by, the population builds up thereby demanding some adjustments within the society. That is what the lawmakers should be concentrating on but they all chose to first fight with the reality as well as fight with the president and one another.

Therefore the president was to initiate a separation barrier, a wall, in an attempt to shield and protect those from the president's hometown, the United States of America. Maybe president Donald Trump thought that a physical barrier might be a great starting point but the problem is not only Mexico as the fact is the problem is all around for everyone was and will still keep looking for a piece of the big pie.

The wall in heavenly terms means changing the society's ideology and shielding the society from the outsiders which is virtually impossible with as many influencers from abroad, near and far, all scouting for anything they could get their hands on at the expense of the poor and the needy from this great nation. Therefore for future interference to the American's business to actually stop, the society has to change and learn how to be an independent society because that is THE WALL this society was asked to build.

Nevertheless, if it is true that there were many outside interferers with the 2016 presidential elections, then the most ironic thing is the fact that, for all of those who were supporting Hilary Clinton in beliefs, body, and mind, through their interference, almost sent the society they love the most straight to the ashes. If it is true that Russians or any other society was interfering with the elections with the intent to bring the society of United States of America down, through their interference they ended up saving the society they hate the most. That was a very close call. You better believe that. Surely almighty power works with wonders for what happened that day was beyond wonders.

I can only let you all now, for I'm just a messenger.

I wish you all well,
Nelson N K